STEP BY STEP

A linked series of Board Books, Concept Books and Story Books
for the pre-school child

Board Books	*Concept Books*	*Story Books*
My House	Colours	Wet Paint
Day Time	Counting	Down in the Shed
Night Time	Noises	Over the Wall
Shopping	Big and Little	There and Back Again

First published 1988
by William Collins Sons & Co Ltd
in association with The Albion Press Ltd

© text Diane Wilmer 1988
© illustrations Nicola Smee 1988

British Library Cataloguing in Publication Data
Wilmer, Diane
    Colours. — (Step-by-step).
    1. Readers — 1950–
    I. Title   II. Smee, Nicola   III. Series
    428.6   PE1119

ISBN 0-00-181119-3

Printed and bound in Hong Kong by South China Printing Co

STEP BY STEP

Colours

Diane Wilmer
illustrated by Nicola Smee

COLLINS
in association with THE ALBION PRESS

"Look at me!" shouts Nicky.
"I've got five balloons."
Red, green, blue, yellow and orange.
"Who wants one?"

"Here you are, Tom.
You have the red one."
"Gurgle-wurgle.
Bloo-hoo!" goes Tom.
"Glad you like it,"
says Nicky.

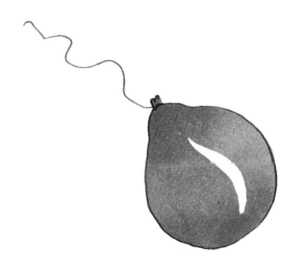

Four balloons now.
Green, blue, yellow and orange.

"Let's keep the green one for Mum."
OOPS!
"Watch out, Mum!"

Three balloons now.
Blue, yellow and orange.

"Dad! Dad!
You have the blue one."
"Thanks," says Dad.
"We'll play with it later."

Two balloons now.
Yellow and orange.

"Yellow for me!"
shouts Clare.
"Yellow like my cupboard."

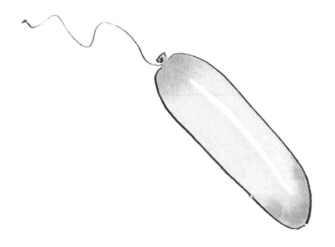

One balloon left.
The orange one.

"Whoopee!" says Nicky.
"The orange one's for me.
Up it goes."

"On no, Kit! No!"
But Kit won't let go.

POP!